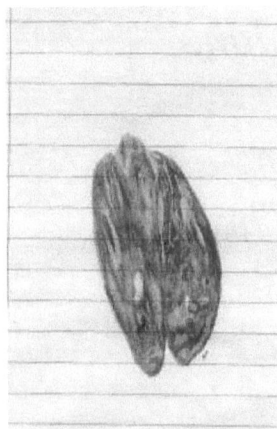

She Sings Unto The Gods Like A sweet Sparrow at Dusk!

Surreal Dreams Three

Ron Koppelberger Jr.

***

Websites
Wolffray.blogspot.com
Farthermostdream.blogspot.com
Snakefuss.blogspot.com
Mirageinblame.blogspot.com
Ethrealsouls.blogspot.com
Horrorrush.blogspot.com
Ravenswont.blogspot.com

<u>Welcome</u>

I am on my third vol. of Surreal Dreams and I want this to be an ethereal experience for those interested in surreal artwork, the artwork of dreams, secret revelation and strange illusion. As with the other books I hope you find something worth remembering or noting in the compilation.....if you do find something here worth contemplating then I have accomplished my goal. I hope you enjoy the following presentation and as always dreams will be served after the show.

Ron Koppelberger Jr. Jan. 2013

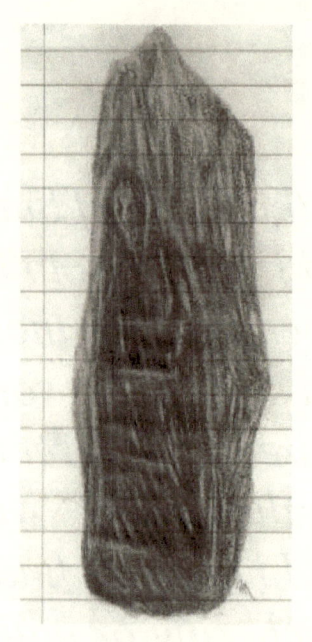

Image Of Doom

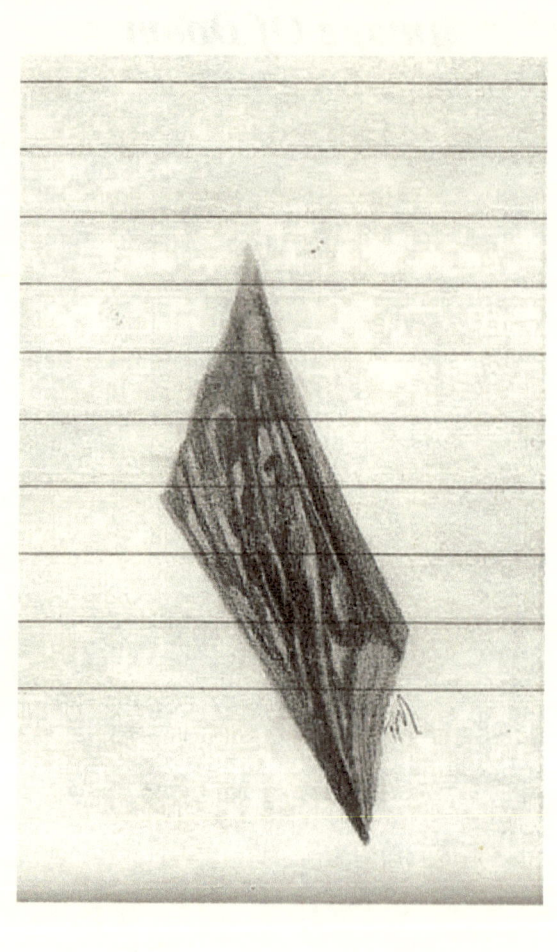

Shy Hands

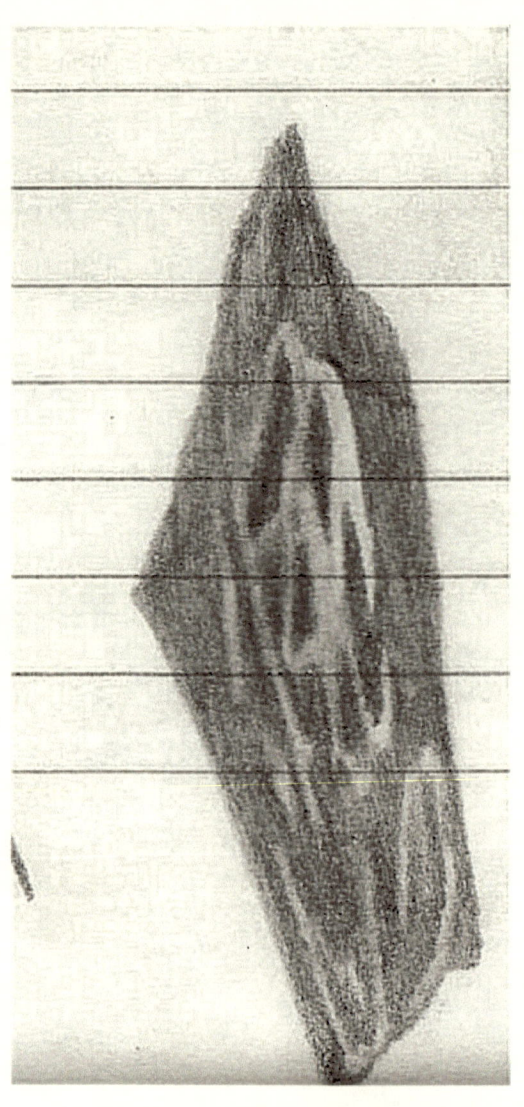

Skeleton Scream

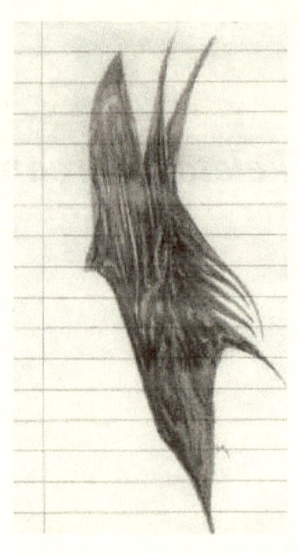

Venus Fly Trap

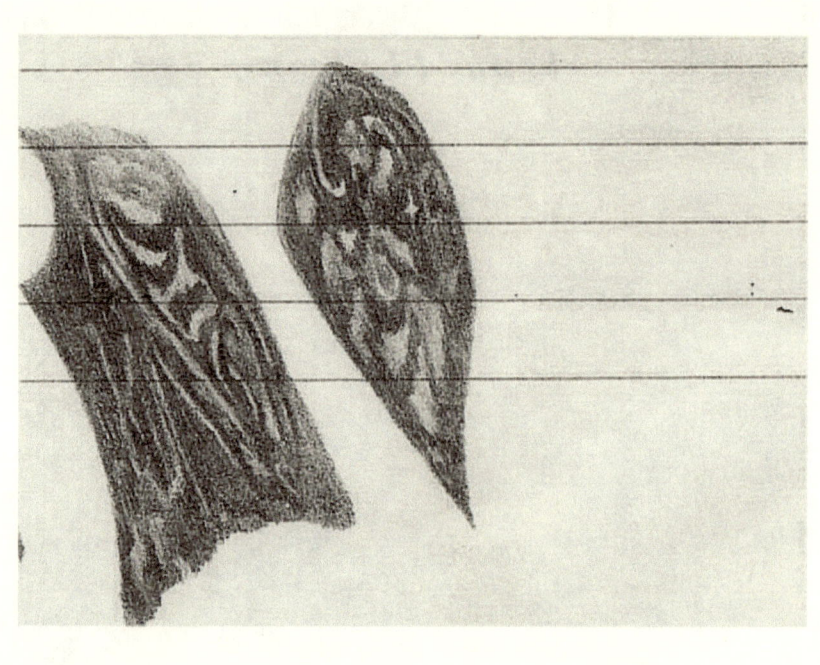

Sage Art

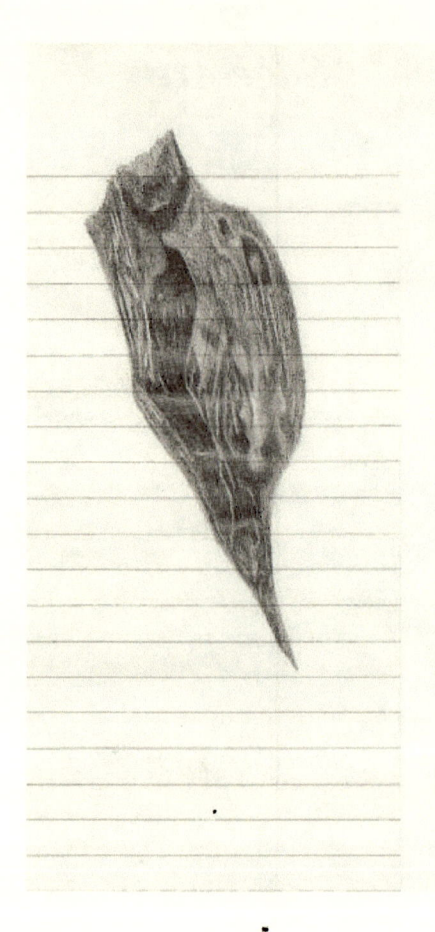

Dark Spirit

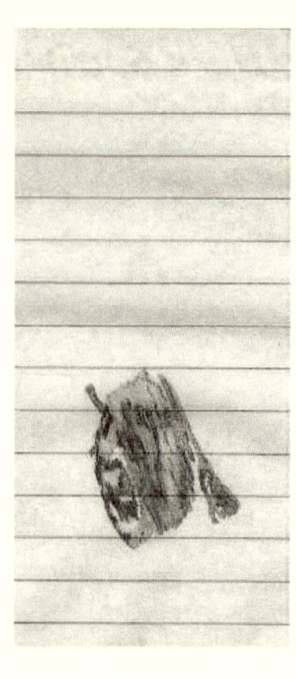

Zombie

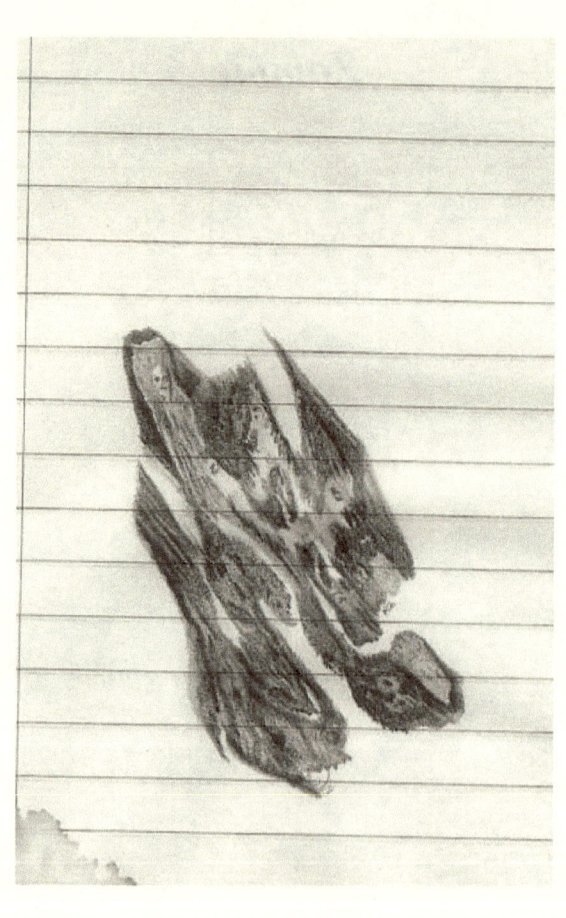

Dreams of Err

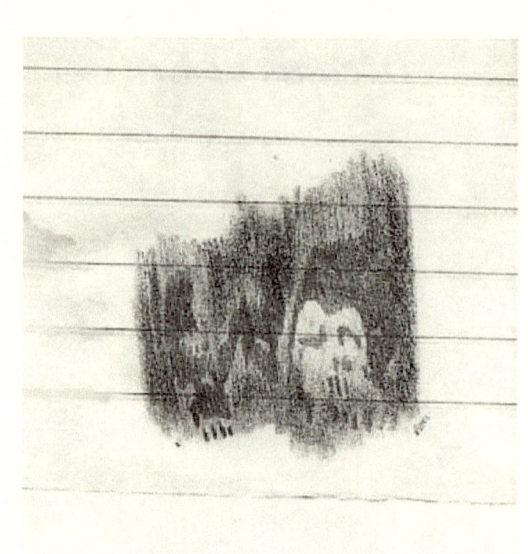

Black and White

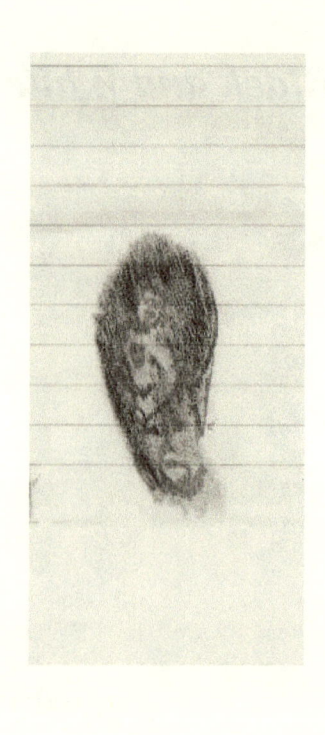

Twins

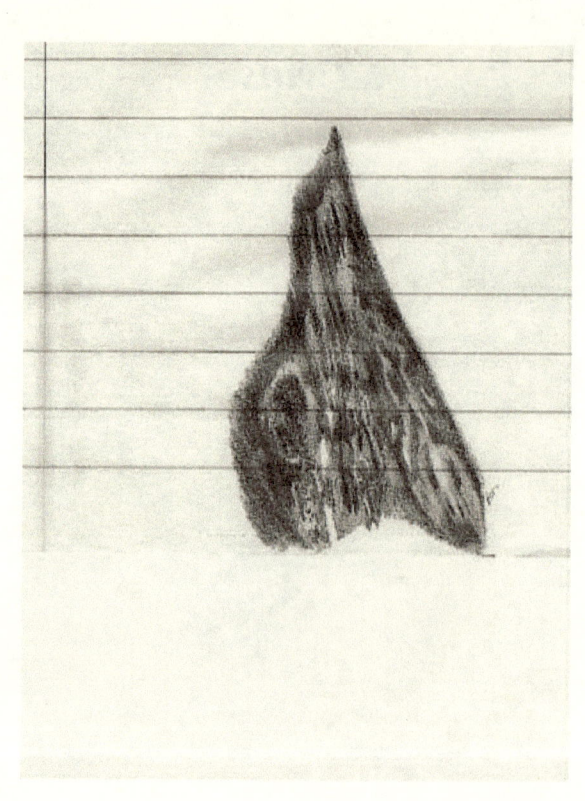

Bedraggled

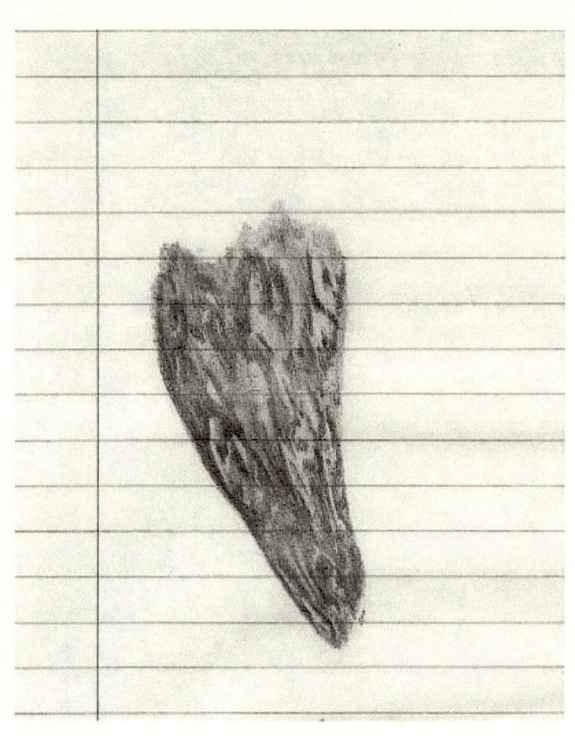

She Sings

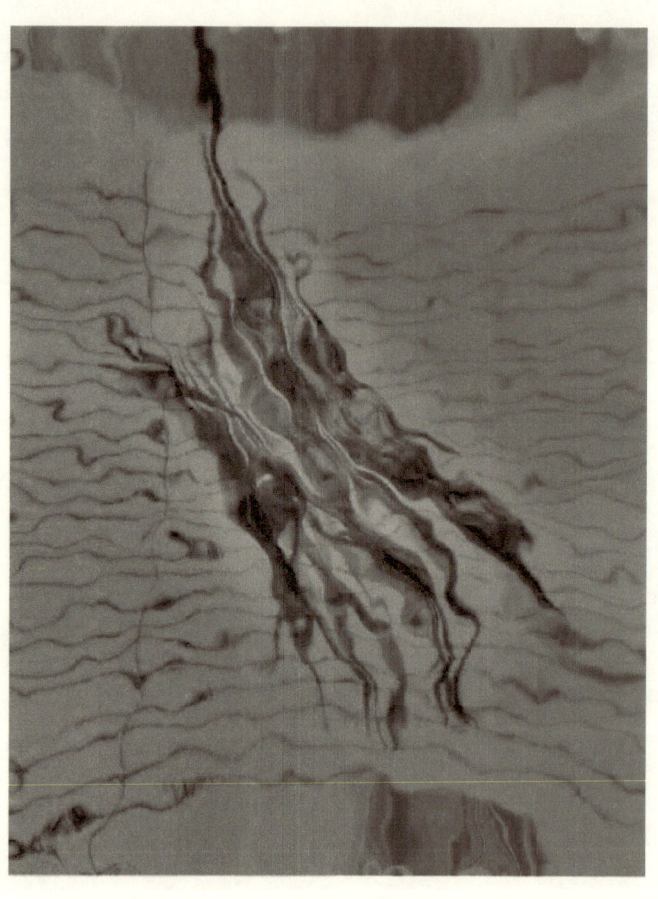

Sting Ray In Glass

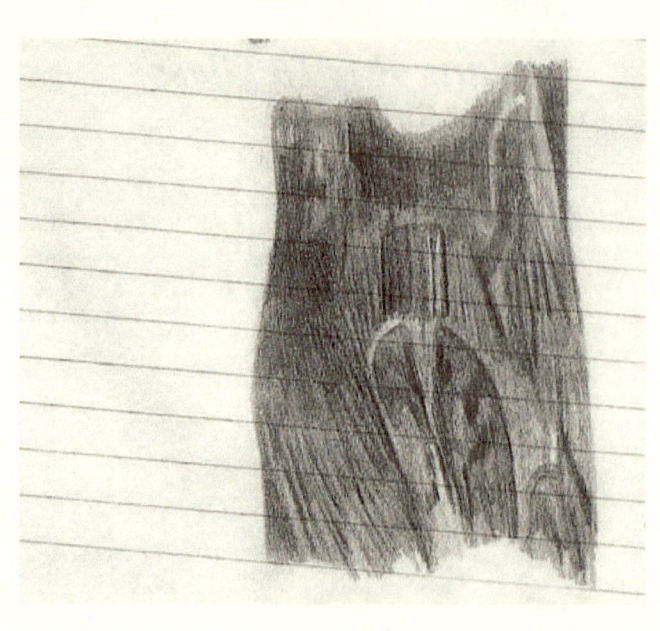

Man In A Cube

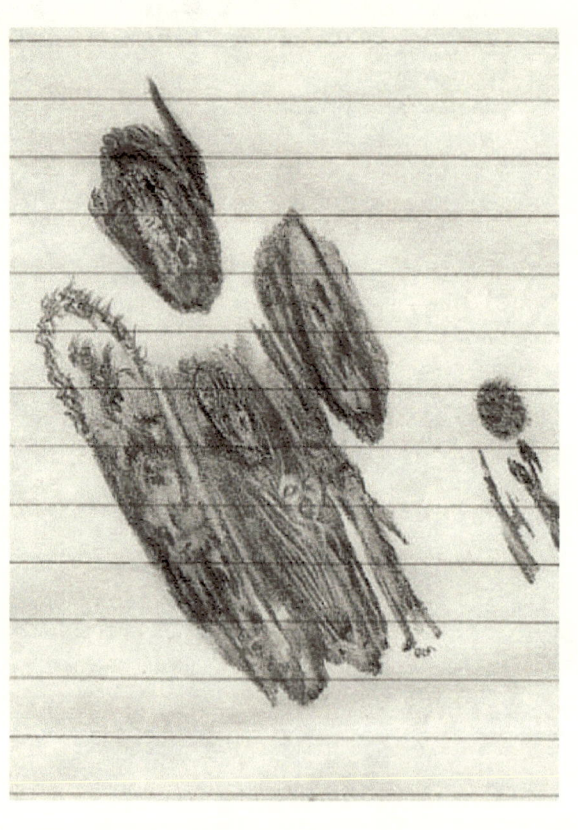

Religions

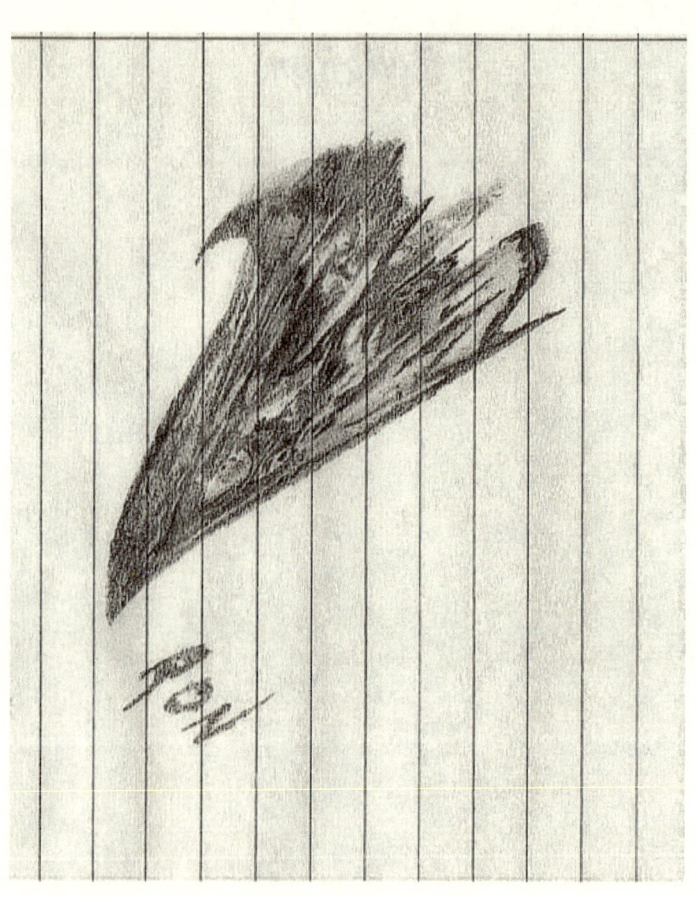

Parchment Secret

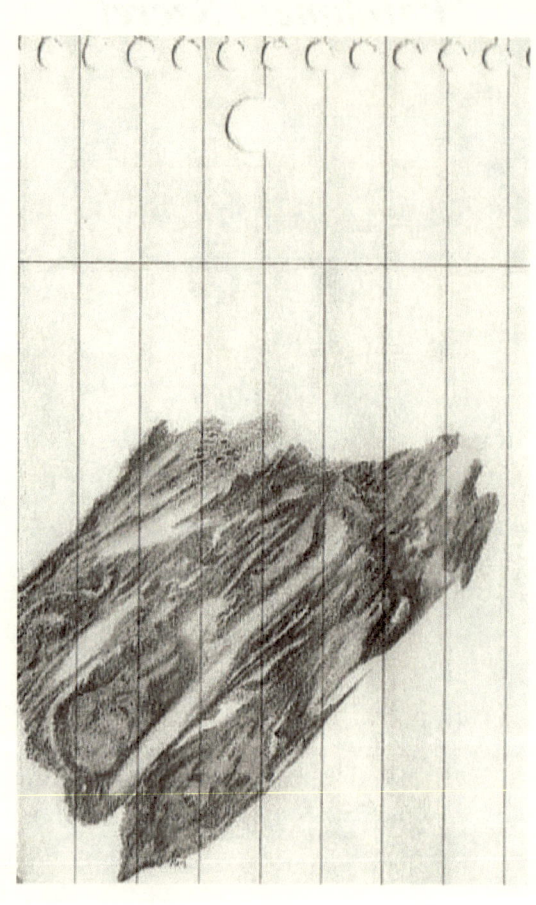

The Vulture

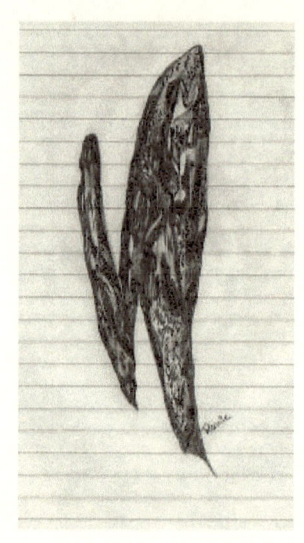

Barbed Wire

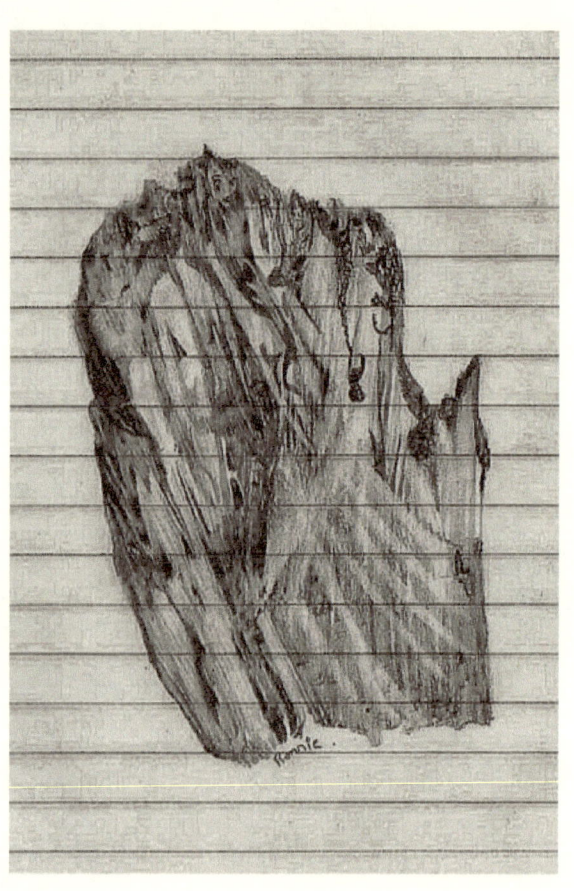

Halloween Preistess

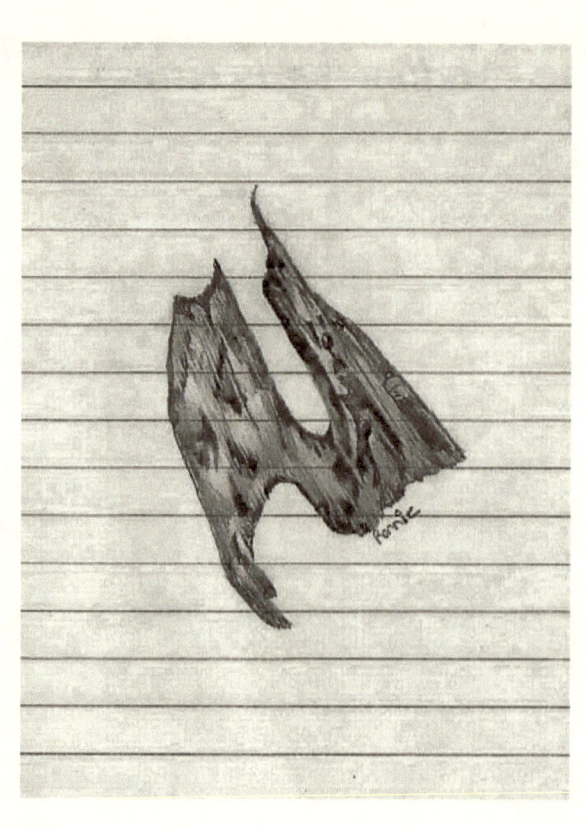

Through The Door To Forever

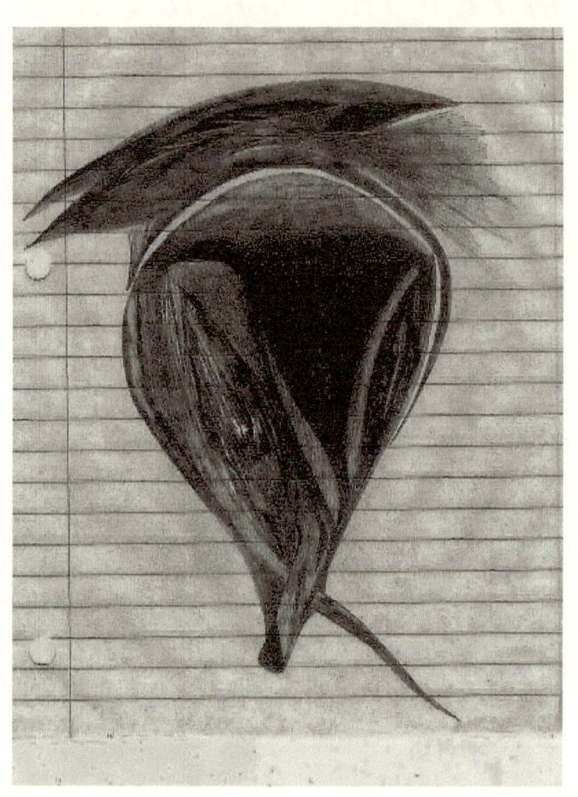

An Angel At Nights Reflection

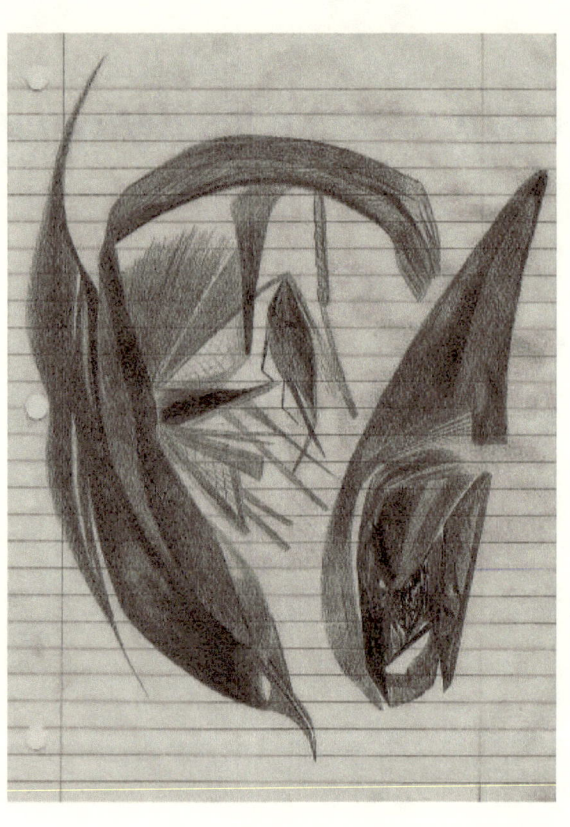

A Cricket

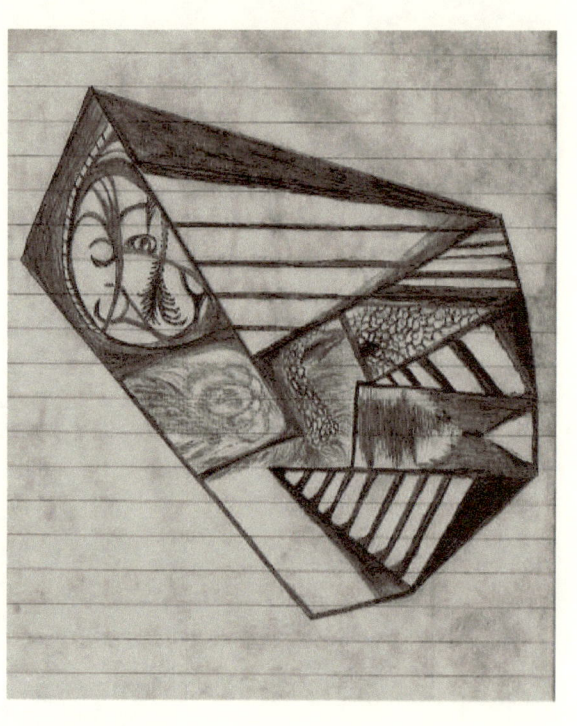

Different Paths

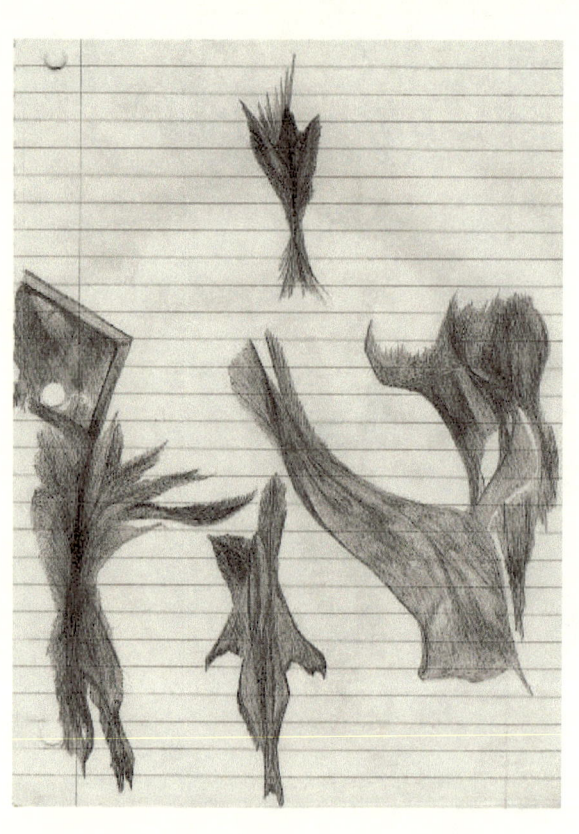

A Parrot

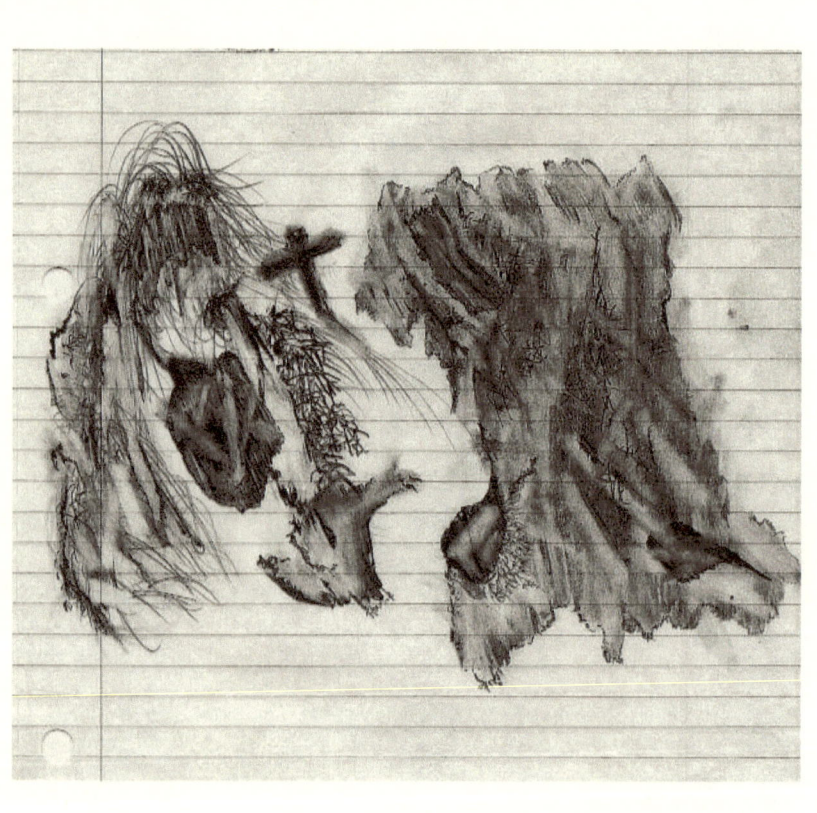

Cross and Wire

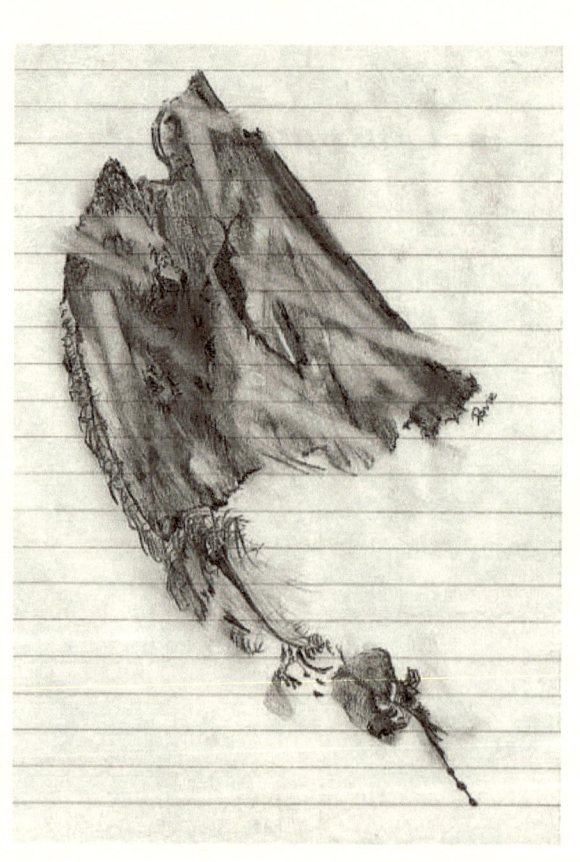

Thoughts in a Blur

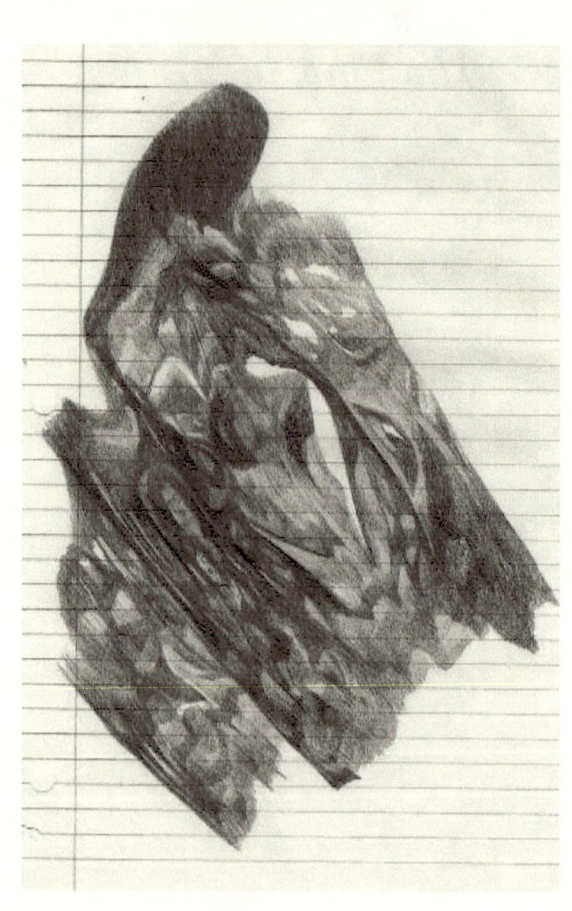

The President

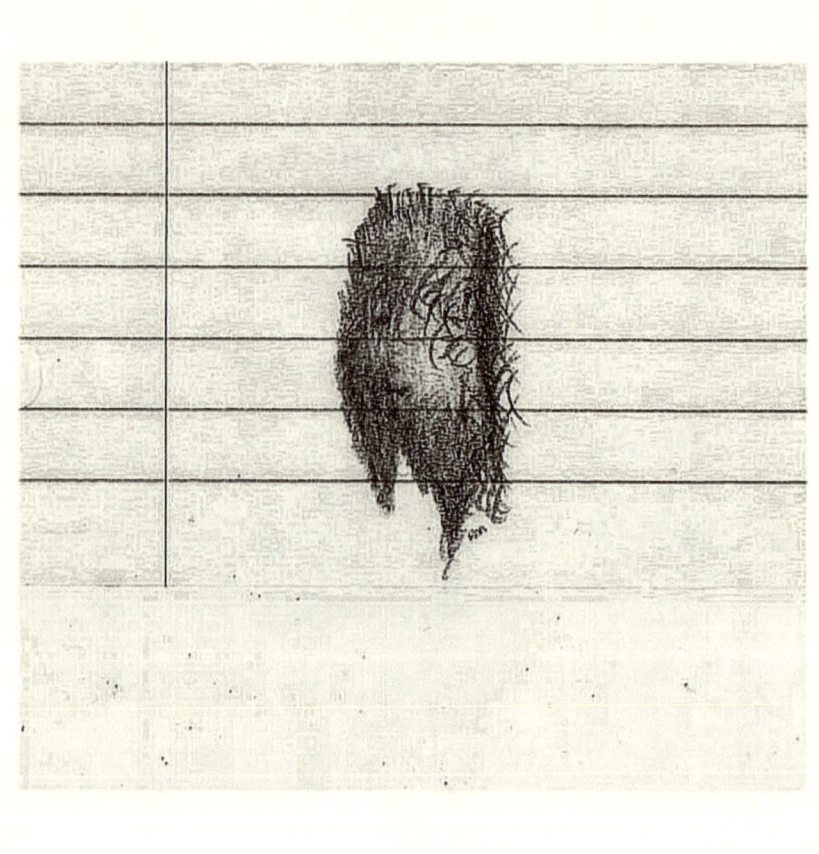

Shy

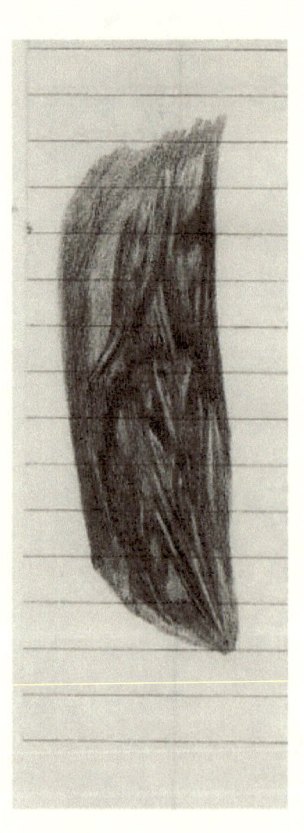

Hiding In Fear

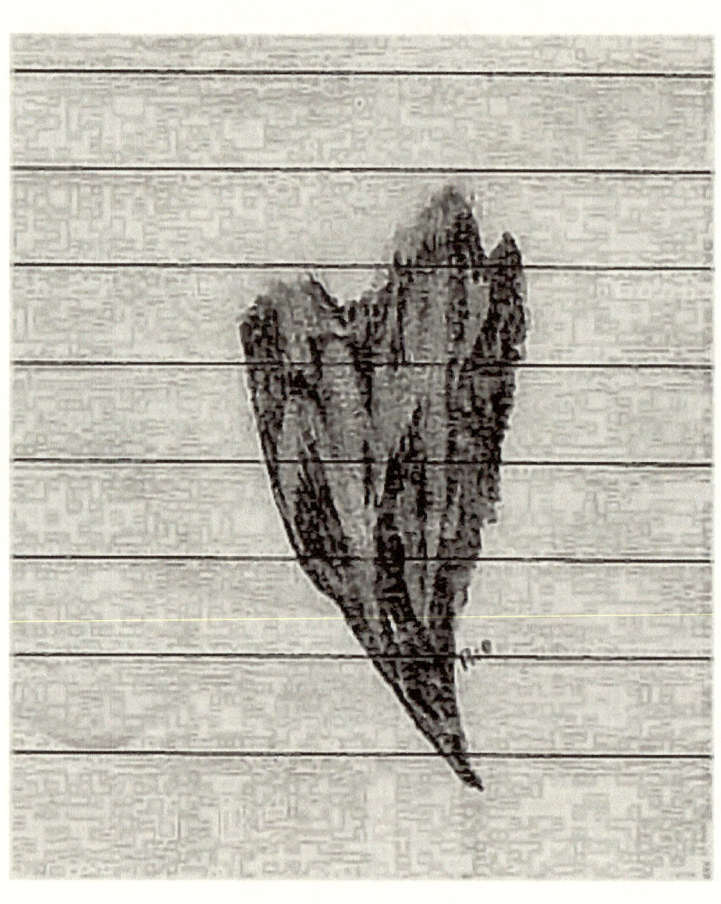

Aged Wonder

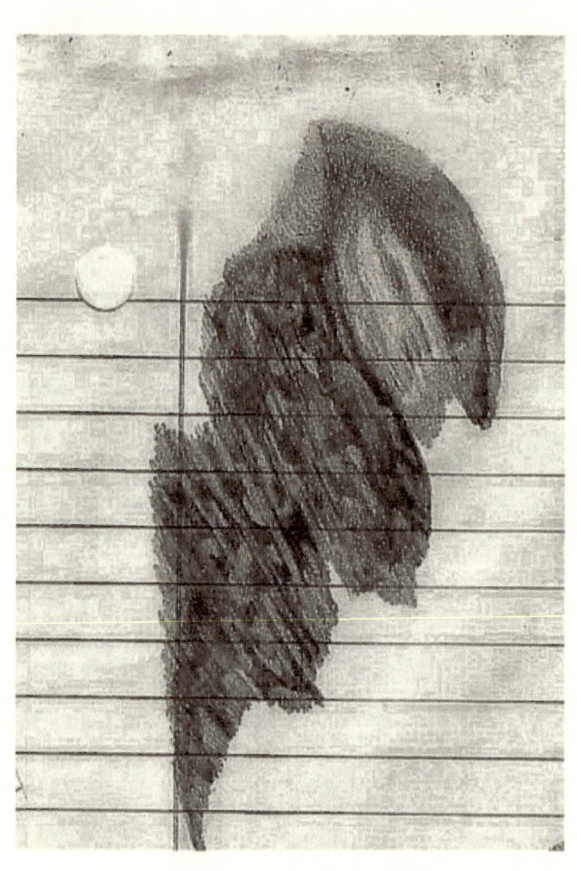

Cherub

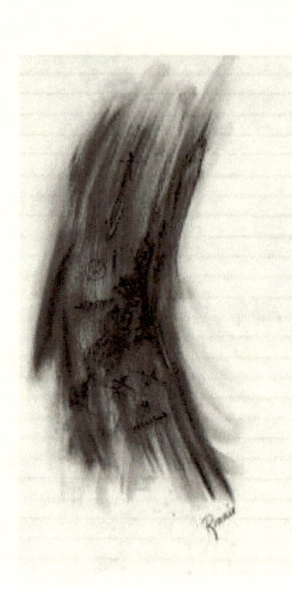

Voodoo Sleep

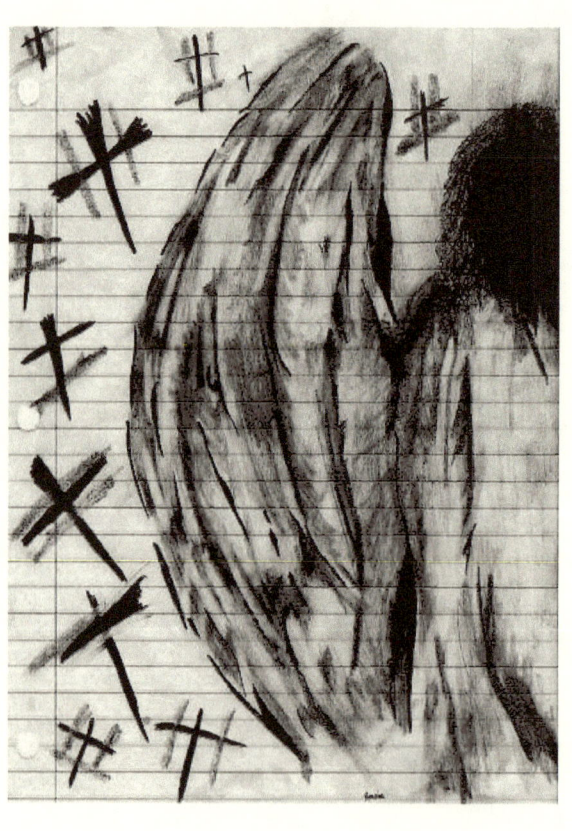

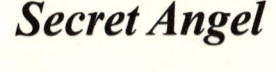

Secret Angel

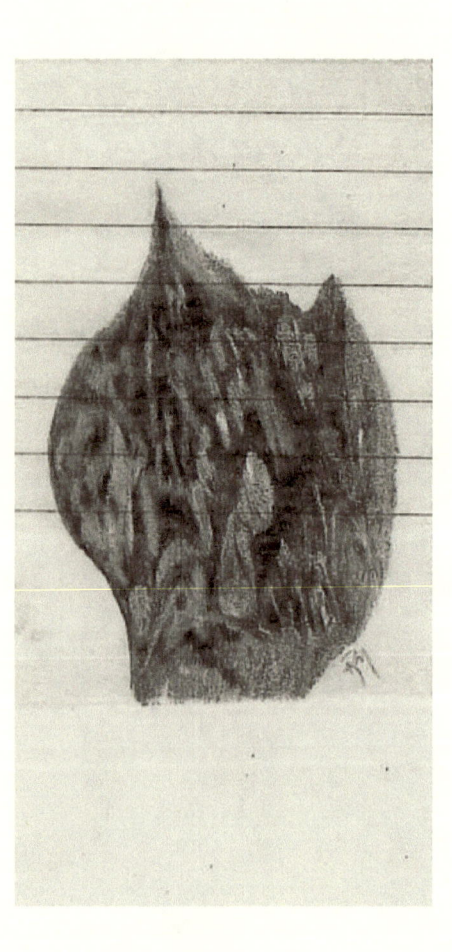

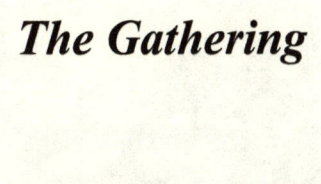

The Gathering

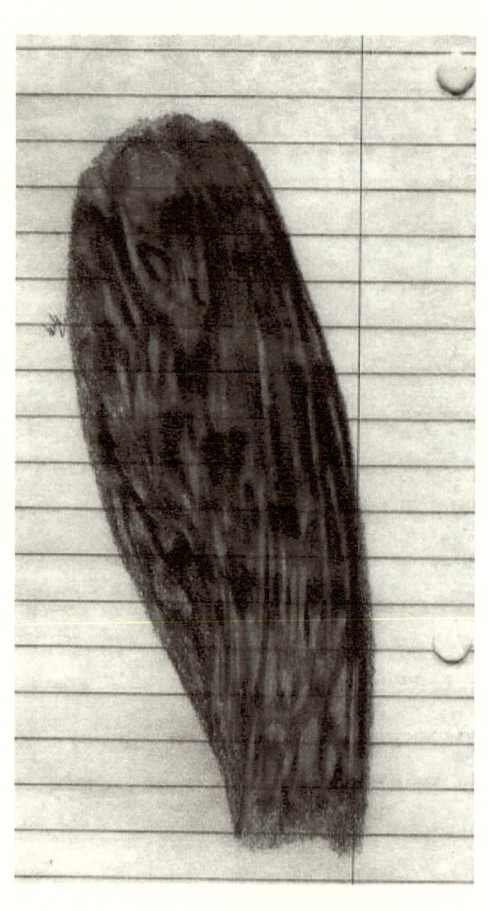

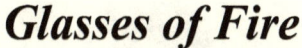

Glasses of Fire

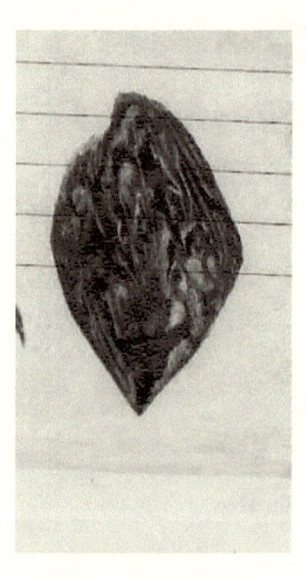

The Grin

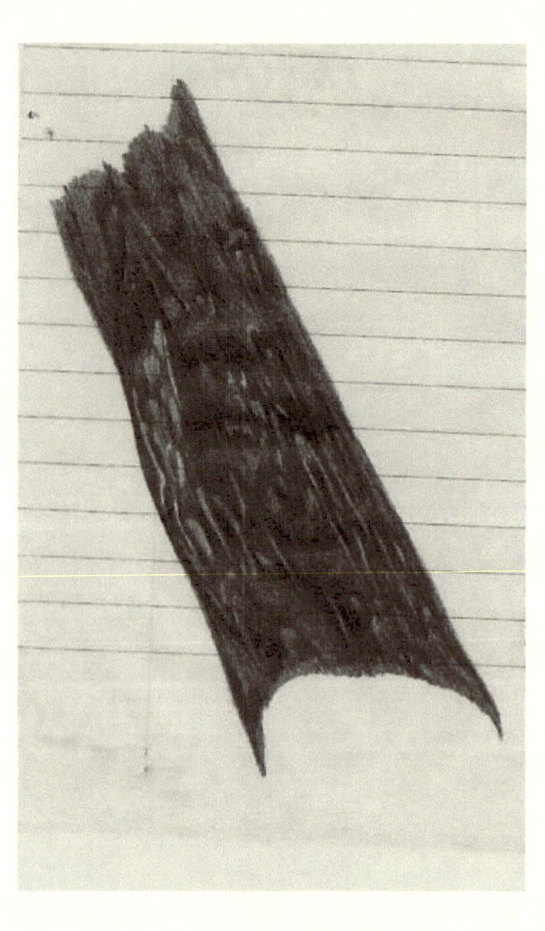

Melding Images of Fate

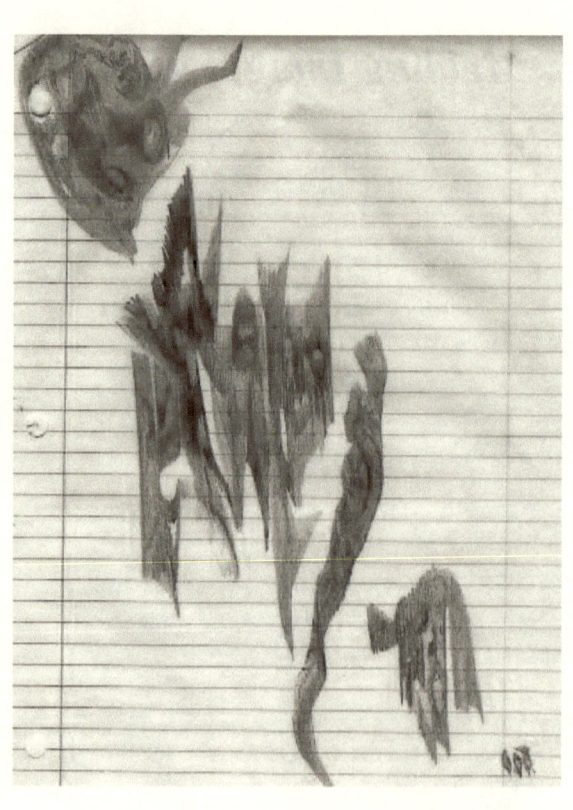

The Wolf

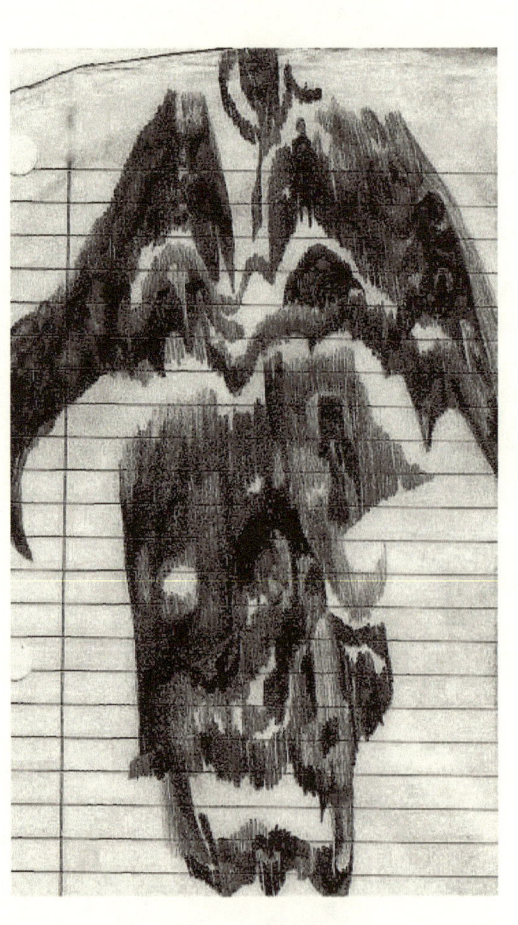

The Pirate

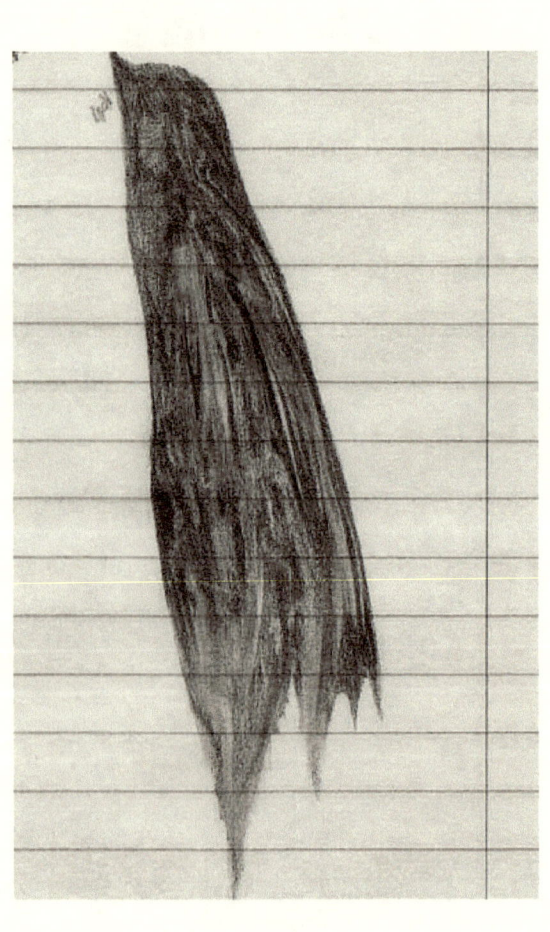

A Curtained Veil

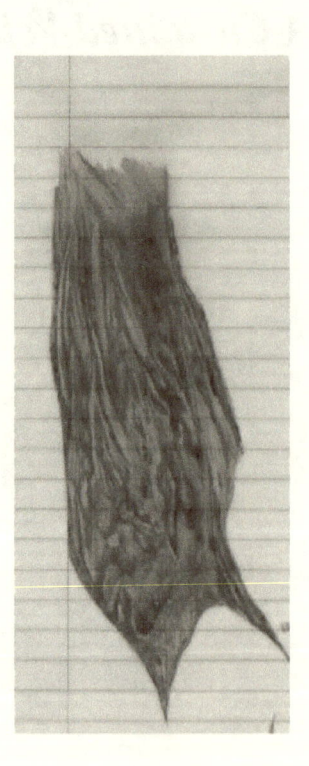

The Devils Veil

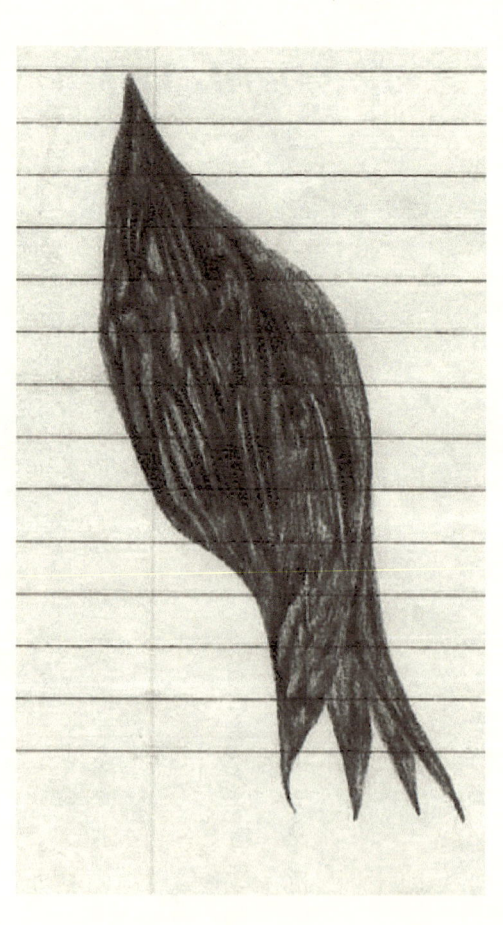

A Greeting

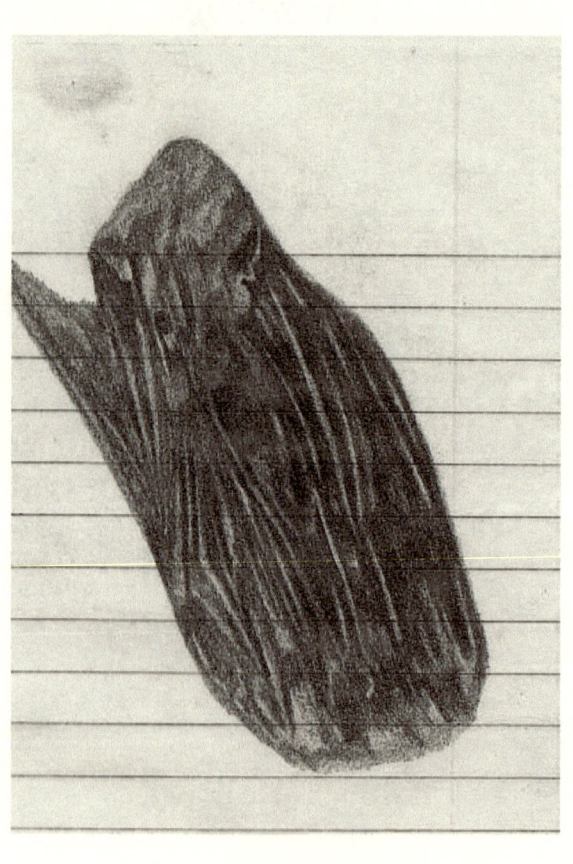

Lost In The Woods

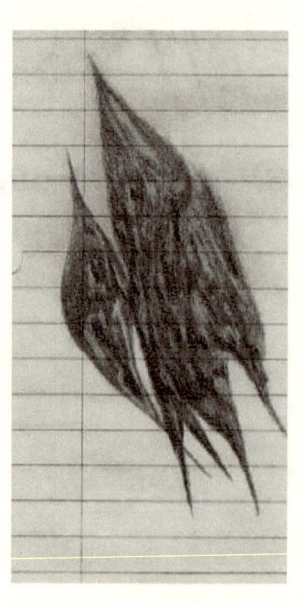

The Gnome

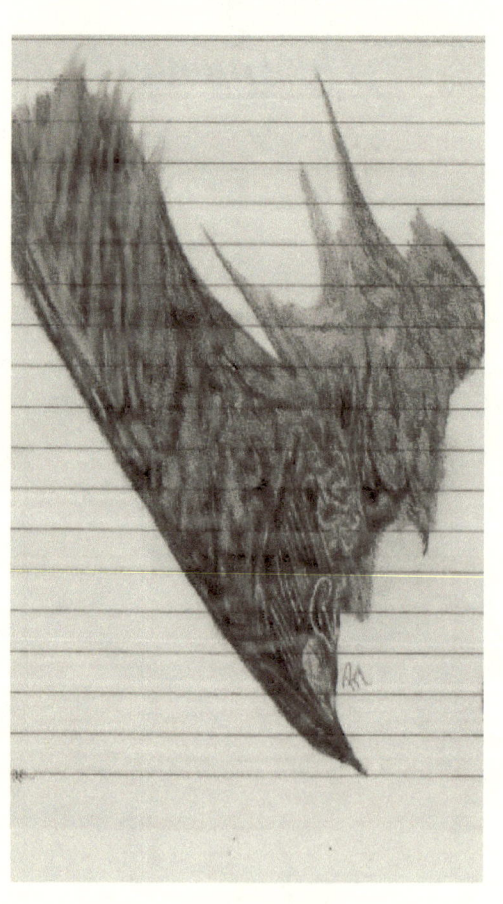

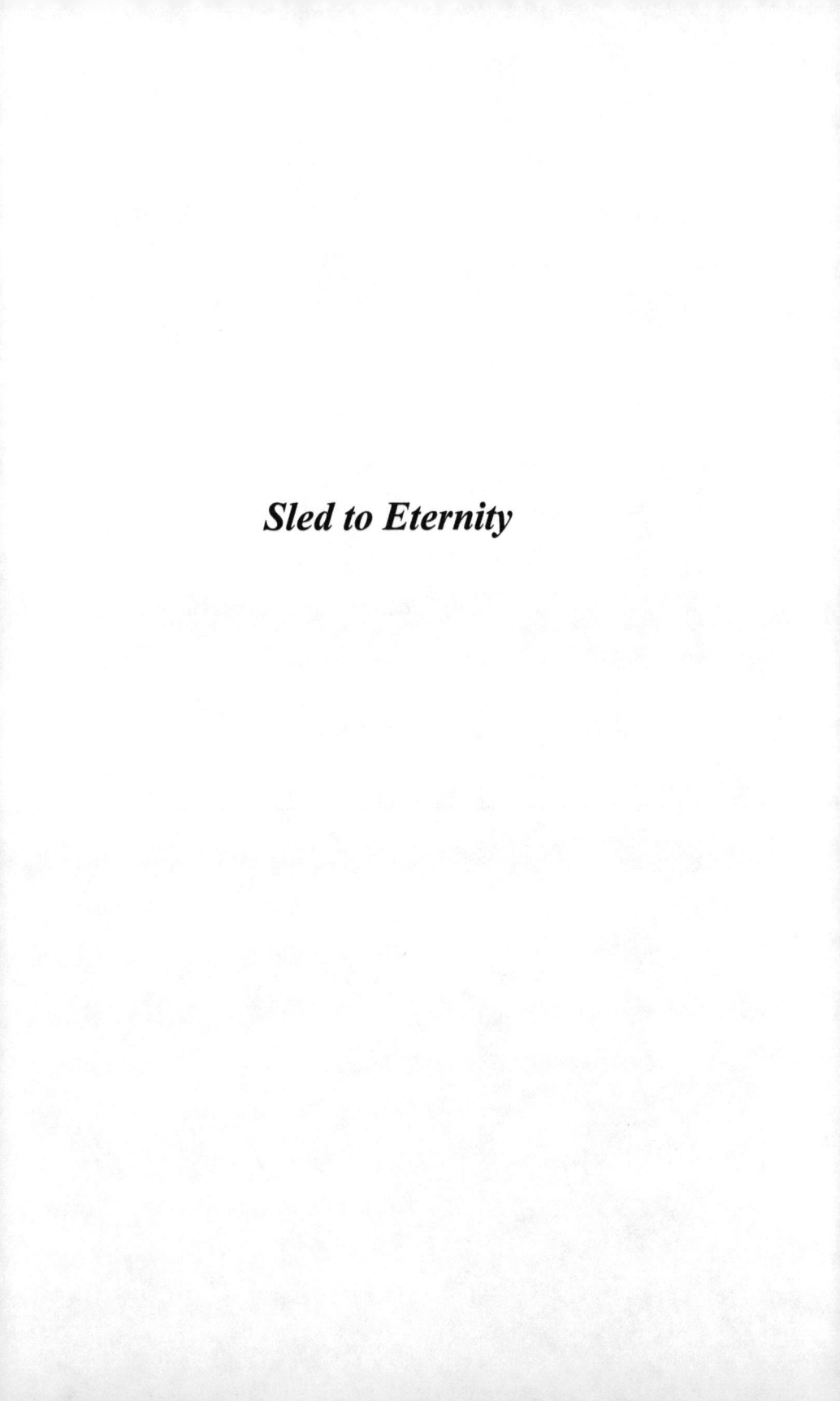

Sled to Eternity

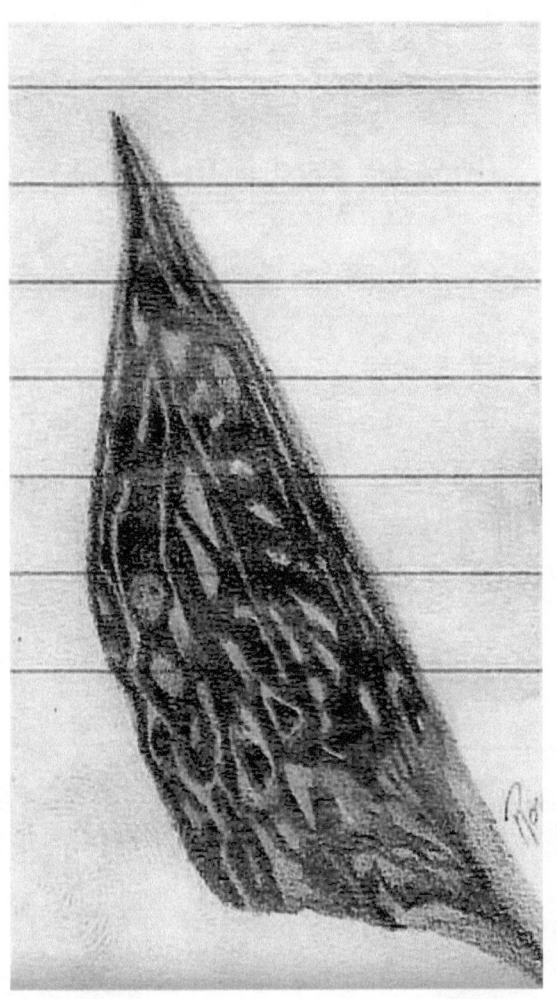

Lost In The Wilderness

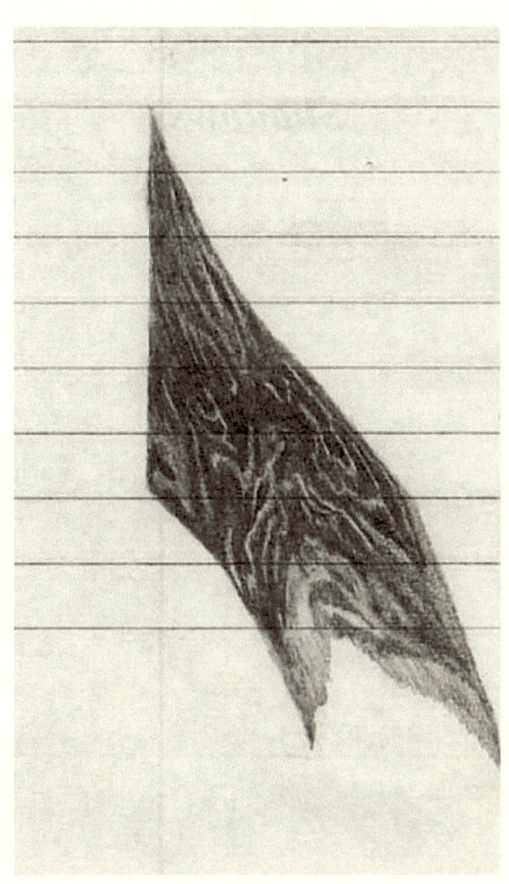

Shadows

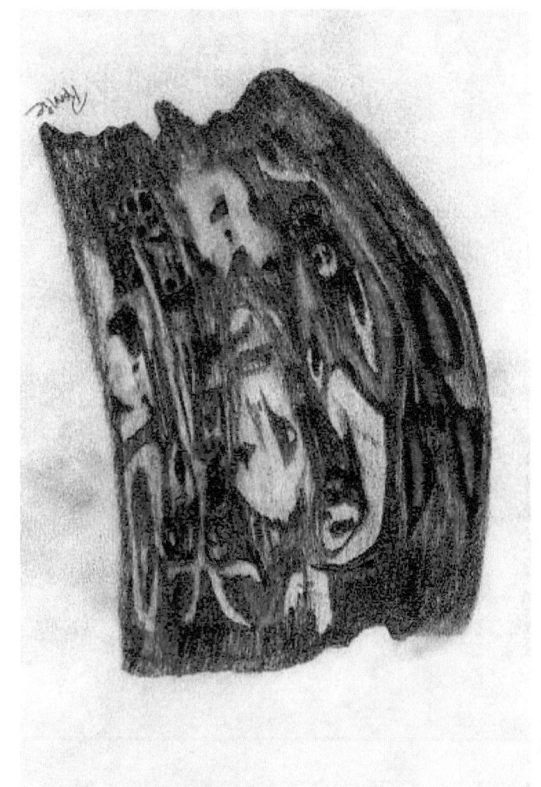

Muscles

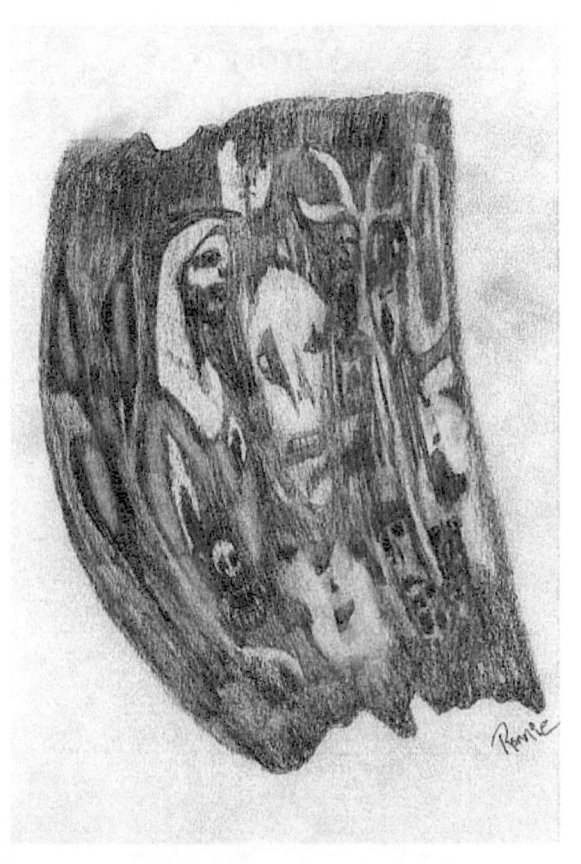

Strong

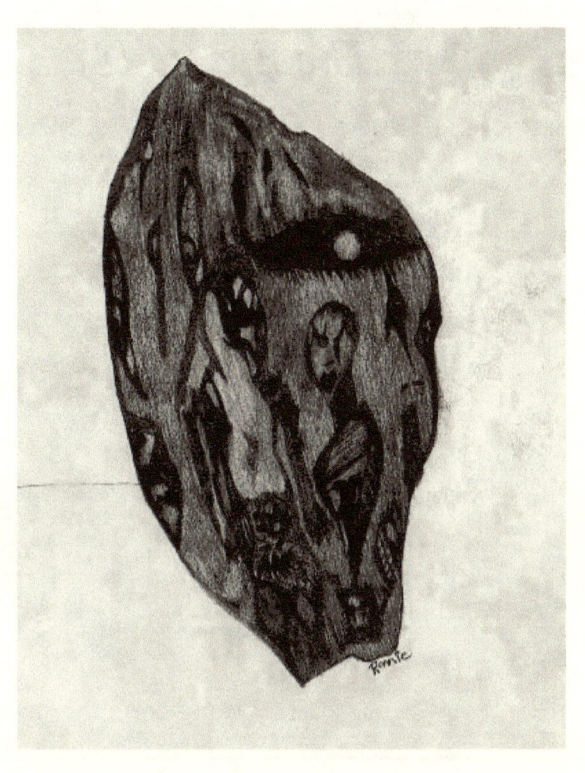

The Eye

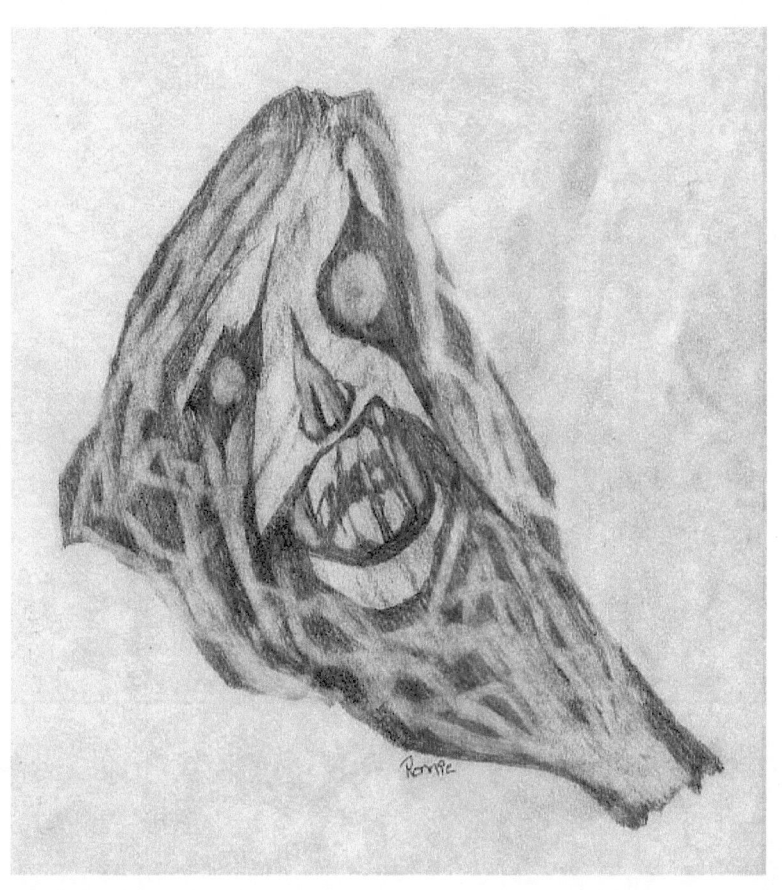

Zombie Eyed

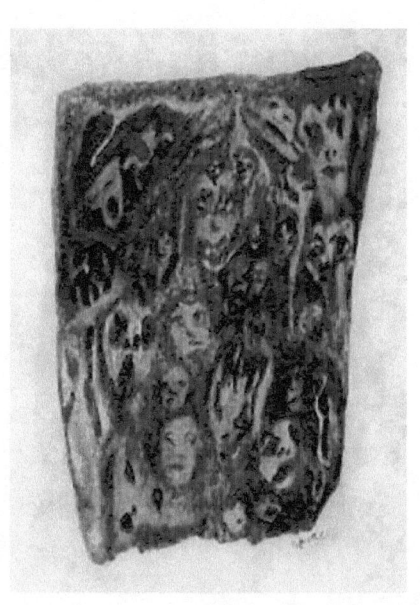

Fresh Dreams And Nightmares

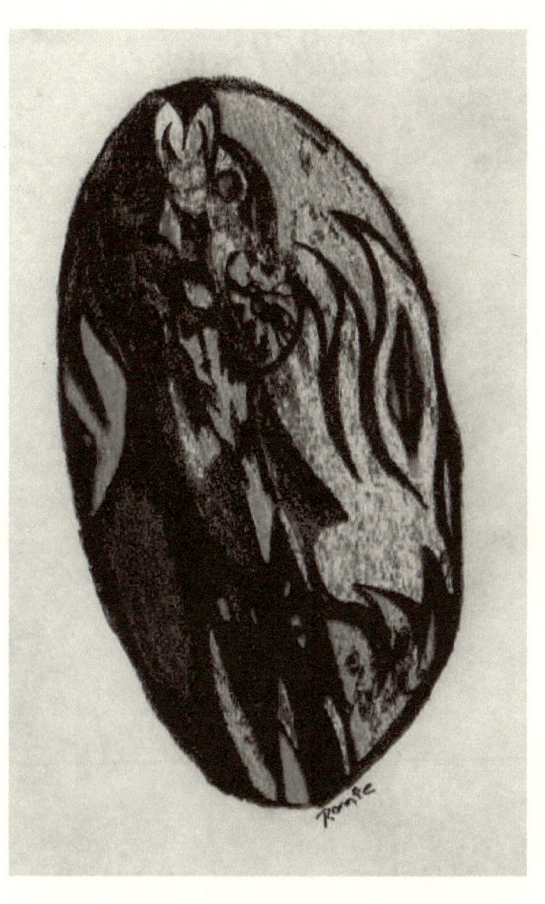

Lady Hawk

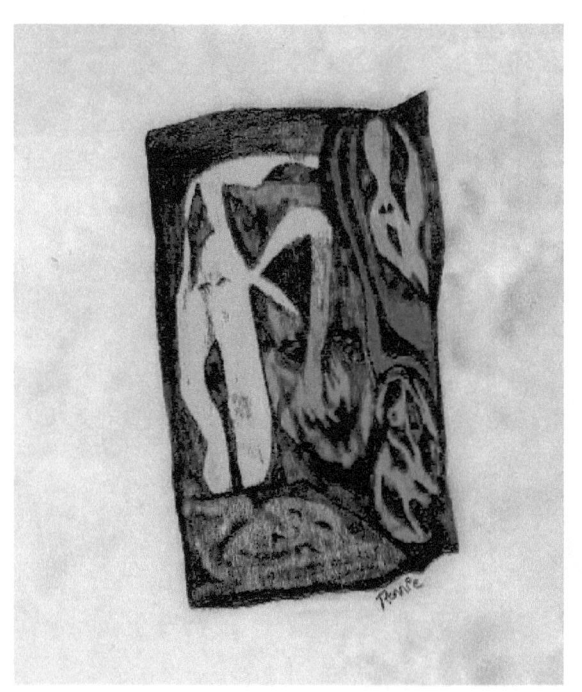

Portrait

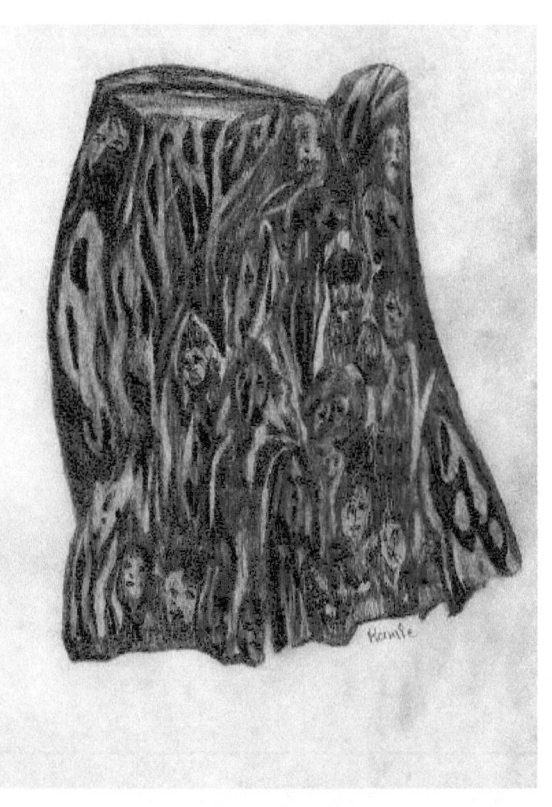

The Gaurds Vision

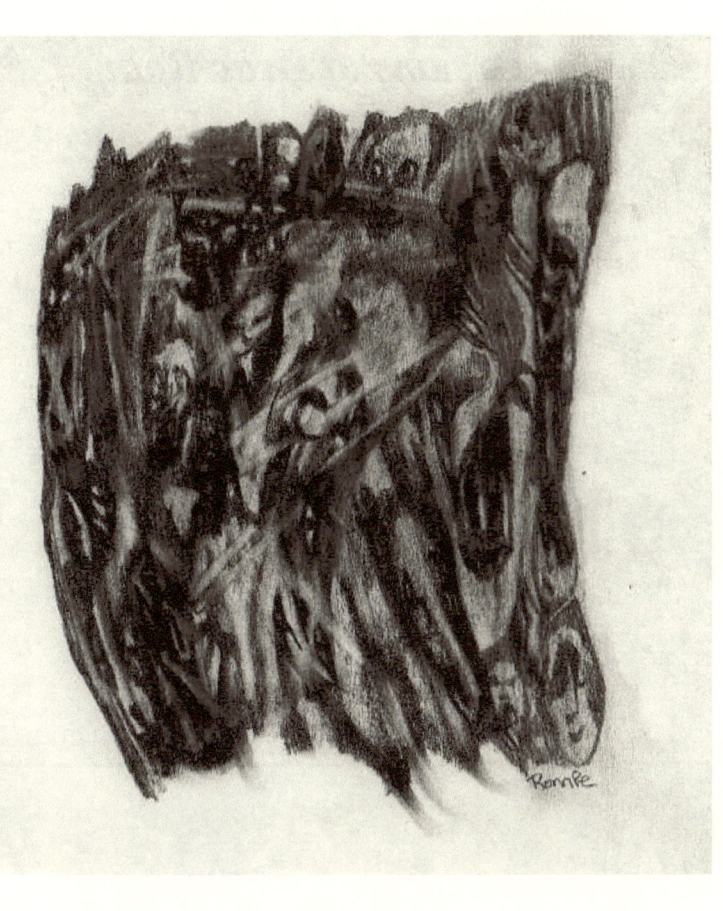

Dreams of Gray Rain

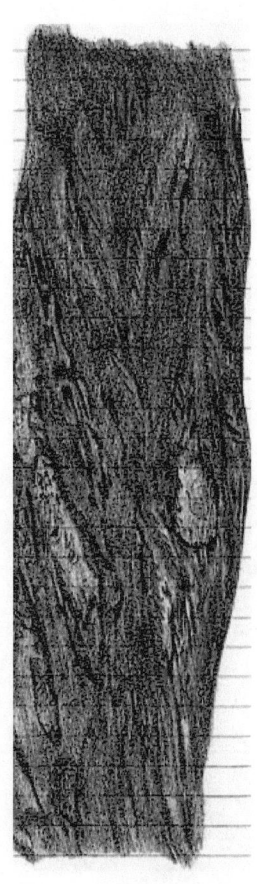

Flames

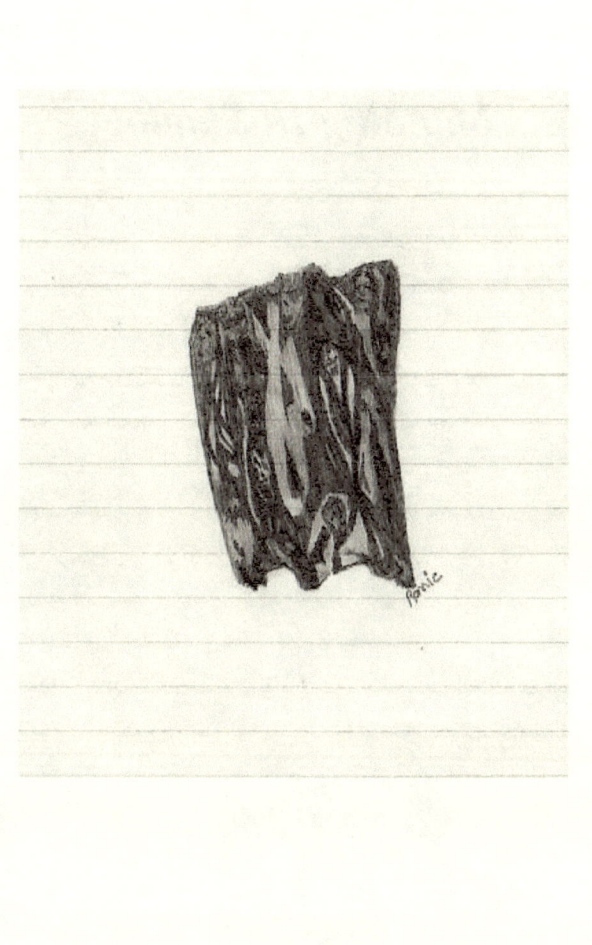

Standing In Shadow

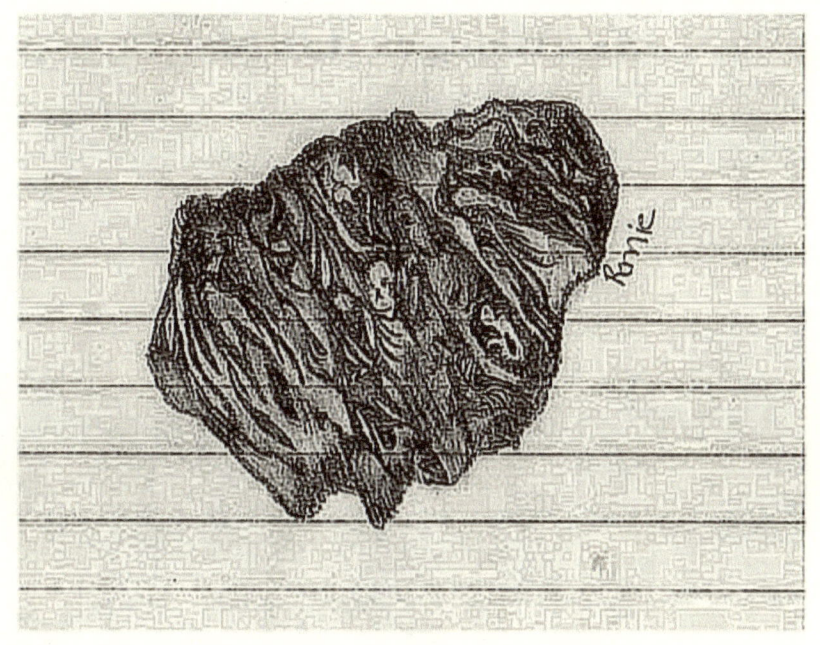

Everything In A Dream

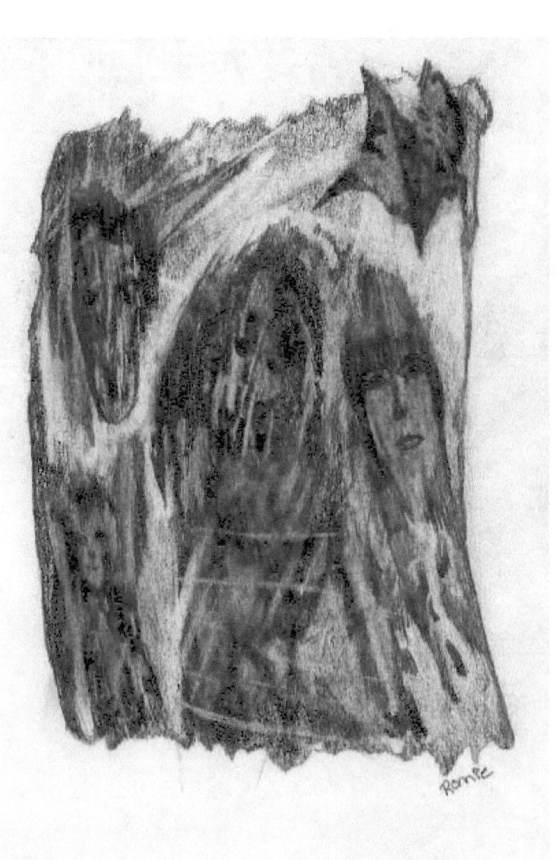

Her Crazy Thought

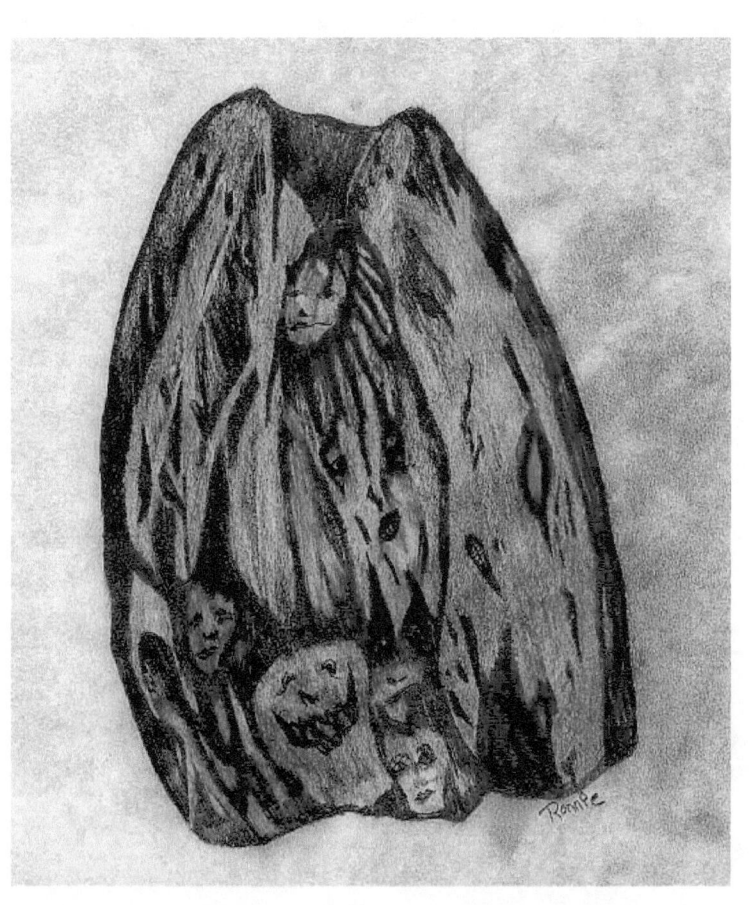

Sun Goddess

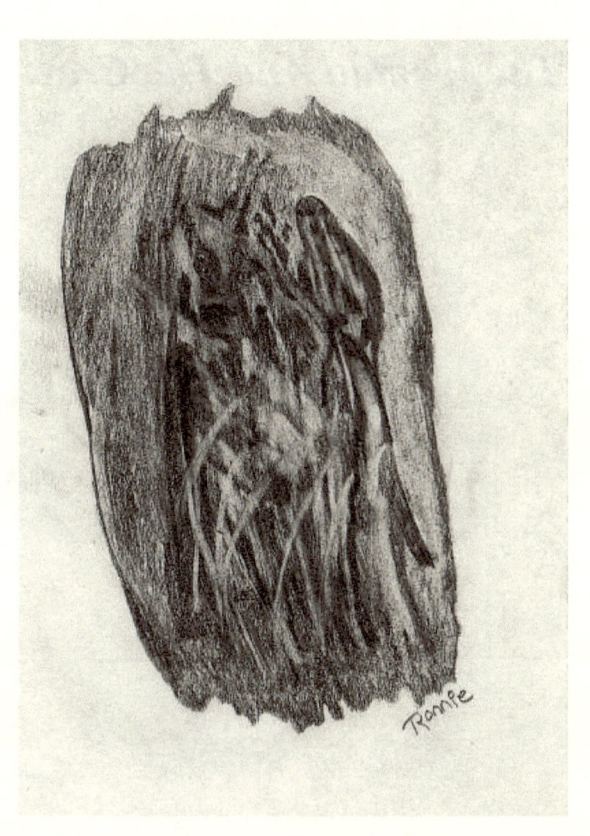

The Woman And The Crow

Thank You for your Attention!!!

www.ingramcontent.com/pod-product-compliance
Lightning Source LLC
Chambersburg PA
CBHW021959170526
45157CB00003B/1054